DATE DUE

ᵤre   #47-0103 Pre-Gummed

Wɔ

Walt Disney's GOOFY JOKE BOOK

Adapted by Barbara Bazaldua
Illustrated by Darrell Baker

A GOLDEN BOOK • NEW YORK

Western Publishing Company, Inc., Racine, Wisconsin 53404

Goofy Sleep Over

Why did Mickey throw the alarm clock out the window?
He wanted to see time fly.

What did Daisy give to the sick lemon?
Lemon aid.

GOOFY

Why did Donald read jokes to the mirror?
He wanted to crack it up.

Why did Minnie say "Excuse me" to the mayonnaise?
It was dressing.

Knock, knock.
Who's there?
Annie.
Annie who?
Annie body home?

Old McGoofy Had a Farm

Why did Farmer Goofy plant seeds at night?

He wanted to grow moonbeans.

What did Goofy call the sleeping bull?

A bull dozer.

What kind of car does Farmer Goofy drive?

A cornvertible.

What's the first thing Goofy plants in his garden?

His foot!

Why did Farmer Goofy ride his horse to town?

Because it was too heavy to carry.

Knock, knock.
Who's there?
Artichokes.
Artichokes who?
Artie chokes when he eats too fast!

Going Nuts

Why does Minnie love to
drink hot chocolate?
She's a cocoanut!

Why did Goofy sit in the
pecan tree?
*To be close to the other
nuts.*

How do you catch a squirrel?
Climb a tree and act like a nut.

What does Donald call a peanut in a spacesuit?
An astronut.

Knock, knock.
Who's there?
Nuttin'.
Nuttin' who?
Nuttin' to do but tell knock, knock jokes.

Donald's Quack Ups

What goes "Quack, quack, slosh.
Quack, quack, slosh"?
Donald Duck taking a bath.

What did Donald say when
he bumped into Daisy?
Oops-a-Daisy!

When does Donald get up in the morning?

At the quack of dawn.

When does Daisy get up in the morning?

At the quack of Don!

What are Donald's favorite snacks?

Quackerjacks and cheese and quackers.

Knock, knock.
Who's there?
Hatch.
Hatch who?
Got a cold or something?

Huey, Dewey, and Louie's Haunted Howlers

What did the boy ghost say to the girl ghost?
You're boo-tiful!

What did Louie fix the ghost for breakfast?
Booberry pancakes.

Pluto's Puzzlers

What did Mickey say when he
thought Pluto had run away?

Oh, dog gone!

What's Pluto's favorite
snack?

Pupcorn!

Why did Donald take a trip to outer space?
To look for Pluto!

hat happened when Pluto allowed a clock?

turned into a watch dog.

CK-TOCK

Knock, knock.
Who's there?
Amos.
Amos who?
A mosquito bit me!

Knock, knock.
Who's there?
Andy.
Andy who?
And he bit me again!

Holiday Howlers

What kind of key can't start Mickey's car?
A turkey!

Why does Pluto hang up his stocking at Christmas?
He's waiting for Santa Paws.

What do you get when you cross Donald with a pumpkin?

A quack-o'-lantern.

Why did Goofy wash his Easter bunny?

His hare was dirty.

What is Daisy's favorite Christmas carol?

"Duck the Halls!"

Knock, knock.
Who's there?
Allie.
Allie who?
Allie want for Christmas
is a knock, knock joke!

Fun Sun Spots

Why did Goofy take mustard to the beach?
To put on the sandwhich is there.

When does Minnie go to the beach?
Only on Sundays.

What kind of fish does Pluto chase?
Catfish.

Why couldn't Mickey make the elephants go swimming?

'Cause they'd forgotten their trunks.

Why did Daisy think the ocean was friendly?

It waved!

Knock, knock.
Who's there?
Ada.
Ada who?
Ada lot of hot dogs and now my tummy hurts.

Goofy Music

Why did Goofy give harmonicas to his rain boots?

He wanted to have a rubber band.

Why was Goofy one mean musician?

He beat the drum and picked on the guitar.

Why did Goofy sit on a ladder to sing?

So he could reach the high notes.

Why did Goofy pack a tuba in his suitcase?

He wanted to carry a tune.

Knock, knock.
Who's there?
Leda.
Leda who?
I'm the leda of the band. Who are you?

Zoo Goofs

What did the kangaroo do when Louie jumped into her pouch?

She got hopping mad!

Why didn't Goofy believe the tiger?

He thought it was a lion.

When do elephants have eight feet?

When there are two of them.

What did the pony say to Donald?

Nothing. He was a little horse.

Knock, knock.
Who's there?
Zoo.
Zoo who?
What zoo wanna do today?

Wheel Goofy Jokes

When does Goofy feed
his car?

At brakefast.

Why did Goofy put peanut
butter on the street?

To go with the traffic jam.

When is Goofy's car not a car?
When it turns into a driveway.

hat did Goofy get when he
ove his car into the lake?
car pool!

Knock, knock.
Who's there?
Tire.
Tire who?
Tire shoelaces or you'll trip.

Knock, Knock.
You're Nuts!

Knock, knock.
Who's there?
Dewey.
Dewey who?
Dewey have to keep tellin[g]
these knock, knock jokes[?]

Knock, knock.
Who's there?
Ida.
Ida who?
Ida love to stay, but gotta[go]
now!

Knock, knock.
Who's there?
Sarah.
Sarah who?
Sarah doctor in the house[?]
These knock, knock joke[s are]
making me sick.

Knock, knock.
Who's there?
Orange.
Orange who?
Orange you glad I'm finis[hed]
telling knock, knock joke[s?]